(put your ~~~~ on ~)
an

I trust this notebook i
safe hands of

~ CHIEF EXPLORER ~

RUSTY

ME

YOU

AARDVARK
WALRUS
CAMEL
PENGUIN
ZEBRA
HANT
TURKEY

" ...The World Awaits You ... GO Explore It...!"

First published in the United Kingdom 2014 by

'Jim Trim Books'

www.jimtrim.co.uk

ISBN   978-0-9929840-0-7

Printed and bound by CPI Group (UK) Ltd, Croydon, CR0 4YY

JIM TRIM
JT
BOOKS

Jolly Jim's A to Z of Amazing Animals

Written and Illustrated by
James Trimm

RACOON

KOALA

QUAIL

Welcome to my home - I'm Jim... *(but my friends call me Jolly Jim!)* - Can you help me?

I'm a great explorer and love discovering new places. In fact, I've been travelling recently around the world and have seen some *AMAZING* animals. But I appear to have lost some of my exploration equipment... well, actually, *ALL* of it!! (...apart from my polka dot pants -phew!) -THEY'RE LUCKY!!

Greetings fellow travellers!

Spot the item that each animal has pinched, using the sticker sheet and place it on the map where I lost it.

....**Uh - oh!!** - those mischievous critters have only torn my notebook to shreds!

- You'll have to unscramble the letters scattered across the page to find the country each animal is from.

MILAAN

ANIMAL!

... Hopefully you can help?! Are you ready for an adventure....??

AARDVARK

Ah-ha! An Aardvark in sight!
Sniffing round for ants
and mites...

SOUTH

FIRST STOP...

AF

GLEN HERALD AIRLINES ...flying you everywhere

BOARDING PASS

CLASS/ CLASSE   ECONOMY

FLIGHT/ SEAT NUMBER/ NO.
241091   07b

DESTINATION
AFRICA

DATE: 08/02/84

Beavers swim;
They dip, dive and dodge,
And collect up the logs
To help build their lodge.

A

ME

CALI FOR NIA

CRACK!

Their big, bright teeth
help fell the trees
Which hopefully,
won't fall...
on me...!!

BEAVER

CAMEL

AF

The sand
is bright
- the sun is hot!

And I am sweating ...
quite a lot.

big, fat
rubber lips to
help eat prickly
cacti

long eyelashes keep out
sand
(not for flirting!)

and HUMPS
to store fat!
(lots of it too!)

flat feet to
walk on sand →

CACTUS

R

CA

I

Dog

gar

me + Rusty

As 'Man's best friend',
a dog is trusty.
I have a terrier –
his name is Rusty.

(Yorkshire terrier)

-den.

my bac k

OUR HOUSE

DOG

He's loyal and playful,
but one thing I pray:
... He wouldn't dig up
my lawn all day!

Savannah sun is scorching hot...
And that's why Elephants
drink a lot!

ELEPHANT

They're slow and steady,
they take their time,
But they jump if creatures
scurry by.